How Firm

From John Rippon's
Selection of Hymns

Genuine Church Music

1. How firm a foun-da-tion, ye saints of the
2. "Fear not, I am with thee; O be not dis-
3. "When thro' fi-ery tri-als thy path-way shall
4. "The soul that on Je-sus hath leaned for re-

Lord, Is laid for your faith in His ex-cel-lent Word! What
mayed, For I am thy God, and will still give thee aid; I'll
lie, My grace, all-suf-fi-cient, shall be thy sup-ply; The
pose I will not, I will not de-sert to his foes; That

more can He say than to you He hath said, To
strength-en thee, help thee, and cause thee to stand, Up-
flame shall not hurt thee; I on-ly de-sign Thy
soul, tho' all hell should en-deav-or to shake, I'll

you who for ref-uge to Je-sus have fled?
held by My righ-teous, om-nip-o-tent hand.
dross to con-sume, and thy gold to re-fine.
nev-er, no, nev-er, no, nev-er for-sake!"

When this periodical is out of print, a license to reprint is available via FAX: 615-251-3727,
E-MAIL: vcopeli@lifeway.com, or MAIL: LifeWay Christian Resources, Virginia Copelin, 127 Ninth Avenue, North, Nashville, TN 37234-0187.

4

We've Got a Rock

(Unison and Two Part)

Words and Music by
DON SCHLOSSER

When this periodical is out of print, a license to reprint is available via FAX: 615-251-3727,
E-MAIL: vcopeli@lifeway.com, or MAIL: LifeWay Christian Resources, Virginia Copelin, 127 Ninth Avenue, North,
Nashville, TN 37234-0187.

6

ask - ing your - self for frus - tra - tion. When you're look - in' for land,_ then the

thing to de - mand_ is lo - ca - tion, lo - ca - tion, lo - ca - tion!

We've got a Rock for our foun -

da - tion; We've got to build on sol - id ground._ We've got our

We've Got a Rock - 4

Wonderful Words of Life

(Unison and Two Part)

Words and Music by
PHILIP P. BLISS
Arranged by Joseph M. Martin

From *Treasure Hunt*, alt. Arrangement © copyright 2000 Van Ness Press, Inc. (ASCAP).

Wonderful Words of Life - 2

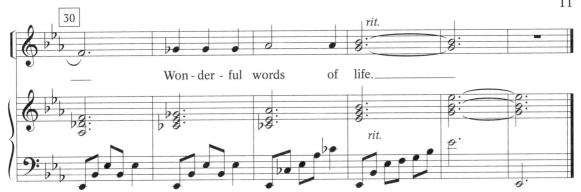

Holy Is His Name
(Three-Part Round)

Words and Music by
DAVID DANNER

*Genesis 17:1   **Psalm 23

When this periodical is out of print, a license to reprint is available via FAX: 615-251-3727,
E-MAIL: vcopeli@lifeway.com, or MAIL: LifeWay Christian Resources, Virginia Copelin, 127 Ninth Avenue, North,
Nashville, TN 37234-0187.

12

praise Him for-ev-er. Might-y is___ His name.___
Shep-herd is___ His

name.___ *3. Ho-ly, God___ is

GROUP 1 *mf*

GROUP 2 *mf*

Ho-ly, God___ is

Ho-ly, Ho-ly; Ho-ly, God___ is

Leviticus 20:7–8
Holy Is His Name - 2

14

Ho - ly, Ho - ly. Bless His name and praise Him for-

praise Him for - ev - er. Ho - ly is___ His name.___

name.___

ev - er. Ho - ly is___ His name.___

On a Day Like This

(Unison)

15

Words and Music Traditional
Arranged by Anita Wagoner
and Don Marsh

Substitute the following (last time only—do all motions in sequence at *)

toot-toot: *Pull whistle.*
oomph-oomph: *Put fist on waist.*
nick-nick: *Stick right pointer finger in the air with arm extended. Stick left pointer down to your side. Turn sideways and stick left heel up.*
chick-chick: *Put fists one at a time over eyebrows or forehead.*
oh-wow!: *Hit forehead with flat palm extended and make eyes big!*

Arrangement © copyright 1996 Van Ness Press, Inc. (ASCAP).

When this periodical is out of print, a license to reprint is available via FAX: 615-251-3727,
E-MAIL: vcopeli@lifeway.com, or MAIL: LifeWay Christian Resources, Virginia Copelin, 127 Ninth Avenue, North, Nashville, TN 37234-0187.

I Am the Way

(Unison)

Based on John 14:6

Words and Music by
JOHN BAKER THOMAS

When this periodical is out of print, a license to reprint is available via FAX: 615-251-3727,
E-MAIL: vcopeli@lifeway.com, or MAIL: LifeWay Christian Resources, Virginia Copelin, 127 Ninth Avenue, North,
Nashville, TN 37234-0187.

Unto Us a Child Is Born

(Unison and Handbells)

Words and Music by
CRYSTAL DAVIS CLAY

When this periodical is out of print, a license to reprint is available via FAX: 615-251-3727,
E-MAIL: vcopeli@lifeway.com, or MAIL: LifeWay Christian Resources, Virginia Copelin, 127 Ninth Avenue, North, Nashville, TN 37234-0187.

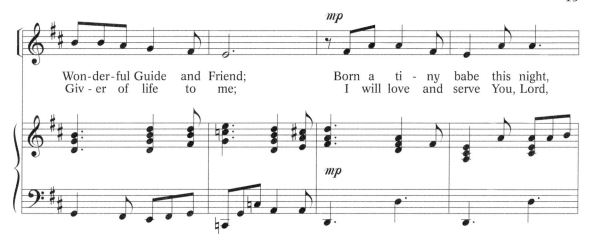

Won-der-ful Guide and Friend; Born a ti - ny babe this night,
Giv - er of life to me; I will love and serve You, Lord,

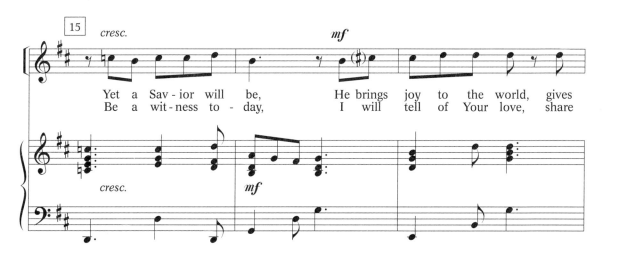

Yet a Sav - ior will be, He brings joy to the world, gives
Be a wit-ness to - day, I will tell of Your love, share

light to all men, And loves me as I am!
hope with all men, And praise Your ho - ly name!

Unto Us a Child Is Born - 2

20

HANDBELLS *f*

There is joy in my heart, for Je - sus is born,

Born in a man - ger with love in His *hand; Shep - herds are tell - ing,

An - gels are sing - ing, "Glo - ry to God in the

Substitute, if desired: heart.

Unto Us a Child Is Born - 3

high - est."

"Glo - ry to God, Glo - ry to God, Glo - ry to God

in the high - est!"

div.

R.H.

Unto Us a Child Is Born - 4

One Bright Star

(Unison and Two Part)

MARY KAY BEALL

LLOYD LARSON

One bright star in the mid-night sky,

One moth-er sing-ing a lul-la-by, One new child in a

One Bright Star - 2

24

Come and kneel in this qui-et place;　Come and gaze　on His

25　　　*mf*

love-ly face;　Come and of - fer the　gift you bring:

rit.　　**30** *f a tempo*

One heart seek - ing the prom-ised King.　One song ring - ing with

hope and joy,　One world a - wait - ing this ti - ny boy,

One Bright Star - 3

One Bright Star - 4

26

dore Him,_____ Christ,_____ the

man - ger stall, And one bright star o - ver

45

Lord.

UNISON

all, And one bright star o - ver

rit.

all._____

rit.

Singing Gloria

27

(Unison and Two Part)

Traditional French Carol

STAN PETHEL

When this periodical is out of print, a license to reprint is available via FAX: 615-251-3727,
E-MAIL: vcopeli@lifeway.com, or MAIL: LifeWay Christian Resources, Virginia Copelin, 127 Ninth Avenue, North, Nashville, TN 37234-0187.

28

Thank You, God, for Your Word

(Unison)

R. G. HUFF and
TERRY D. TAYLOR

TERRY D. TAYLOR

Thank You, God,_ for_ Your Word, words to be spo - ken and sung! Thank You, God,_ for_ _ Your Word, words to re - mem - ber, words to_ be

Second time to Coda

When this periodical is out of print, a license to reprint is available via FAX: 615-251-3727,
E-MAIL: vcopeli@lifeway.com, or MAIL: LifeWay Christian Resources, Virginia Copelin, 127 Ninth Avenue, North,
Nashville, TN 37234-0187.

Thank You, God, for Your Word - 2

I'm Being Built Up

(Unison)

Words and Music by
DON SCHLOSSER

Shuffle (♩ = 140)

UNISON

(hammer taps)

I'm be-ing built up to trust in the Lord; I'm be-ing built up to fol-low His Word. I'm be-ing built up, built up, built up; Yes, I'm un-der con-struc-tion for the King-dom of God. I'm be-ing

When this periodical is out of print, a license to reprint is available via FAX: 615-251-3727,
E-MAIL: vcopeli@lifeway.com, or MAIL: LifeWay Christian Resources, Virginia Copelin, 127 Ninth Avenue, North,
Nashville, TN 37234-0187.

33

I'm Being Built Up - 2

34